Before They Were President

BEFORE ANDREW JACKSON WAS PRESIDENT

Gareth Stevens
PUBLISHING

By Michael Rajczak

Please visit our website, www.garethstevens.com. For a free color catalog of all our high-quality books, call toll free 1-800-542-2595 or fax 1-877-542-2596.

Library of Congress Cataloging-in-Publication Data

Names: Rajczak, Michael, author.
Title: Before Andrew Jackson was president / Michael Rajczak.
Description: New York : Gareth Stevens Publishing, 2018. | Series: Before they were president | Includes index.
Identifiers: LCCN 2017022999| ISBN 9781538210604 (pbk.) | ISBN 9781538210611 (6 pack) | ISBN 9781538210628 (library bound)
Subjects: LCSH: Jackson, Andrew, 1767-1845–Juvenile literature. |
  Presidents–United States–Biography–Juvenile literature.
Classification: LCC E382 .R23 2018 | DDC 973.56092 [B] –dc23
LC record available at https://lccn.loc.gov/2017022999

First Edition

Published in 2018 by
Gareth Stevens Publishing
111 East 14th Street, Suite 349
New York, NY 10003

Copyright © 2018 Gareth Stevens Publishing

Designer: Laura Bowen
Editor: Ryan Nagelhout/Kate Mikoley

Photo credits: Cover, p. 1 (Andrew Jackson) Universal Images Group/Getty Images; cover, p. 1 (battle scene) Bettmann/Getty Images; cover, pp. 1–21 (frame) Samran wonglakorn/Shutterstock.com; p. 5 Interim Archives/ Getty Images; p. 7 digidreamgrafix/Shutterstock.com; pp. 9, 21 (The Hermitage) File Upload Bot (Magnus Manske)/ Wikimedia Commons; p. 13 Stock Montage/Archive Photos/Getty Images; p. 15 Popperfoto/Getty Images; p. 17 (main) Courtesty of Library of Congress; p. 17 (inset) Nik Keevil/Shutterstock.com; pp. 19, 21 (Andrew Jackson) Everett Historical/Shutterstock.com.

Printed in China

CPSIA compliance information: Batch #CW18GS: For further information contact Gareth Stevens, New York, New York at 1-800-542-2595.

CONTENTS

Words in the glossary appear in **bold** type the first time they are used in the text.

AN IMMIGRANT FAMILY

When Andrew Jackson became president, he was a wealthy man with many accomplishments. But his life began quite simply. About 2 years before his birth, Jackson's family came to the United States from northern Ireland.

The family hoped to start a farm in the Waxhaws area of the Carolinas, which is near the border between North and South Carolina. Shortly before Andrew was born, his father died in an accident. Jackson's mother, Elizabeth, and her three young boys moved in with her sister's family.

Presidential Preview

Andrew Jackson was named after his father, who died in 1767, just weeks before Andrew was born.

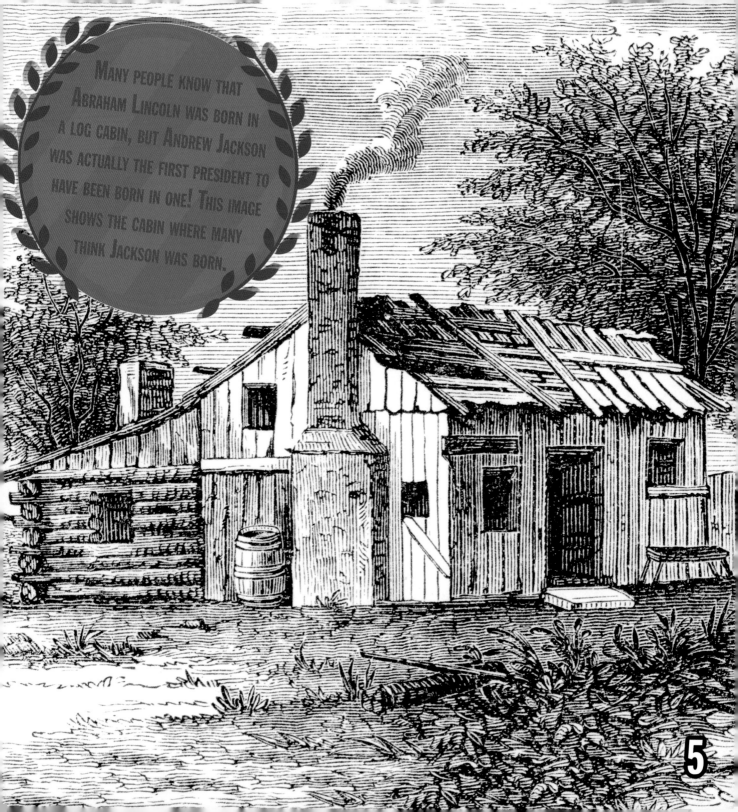

Many people know that Abraham Lincoln was born in a log cabin, but Andrew Jackson was actually the first president to have been born in one! This image shows the cabin where many think Jackson was born.

5

GROWING UP IN THE WAXHAWS

Elizabeth's sister and her husband had a large family of their own. When Andrew was old enough, he helped his uncle on the farm. He was growing into a strong, tall boy with a mop of fire-red hair.

Although he was a very good reader, Andrew didn't like school. He preferred to skip class and play with his friends. Andrew became known for playing jokes and fighting. He would rather race on horseback than study.

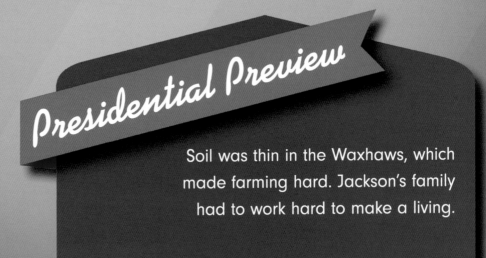

Presidential Preview

Soil was thin in the Waxhaws, which made farming hard. Jackson's family had to work hard to make a living.

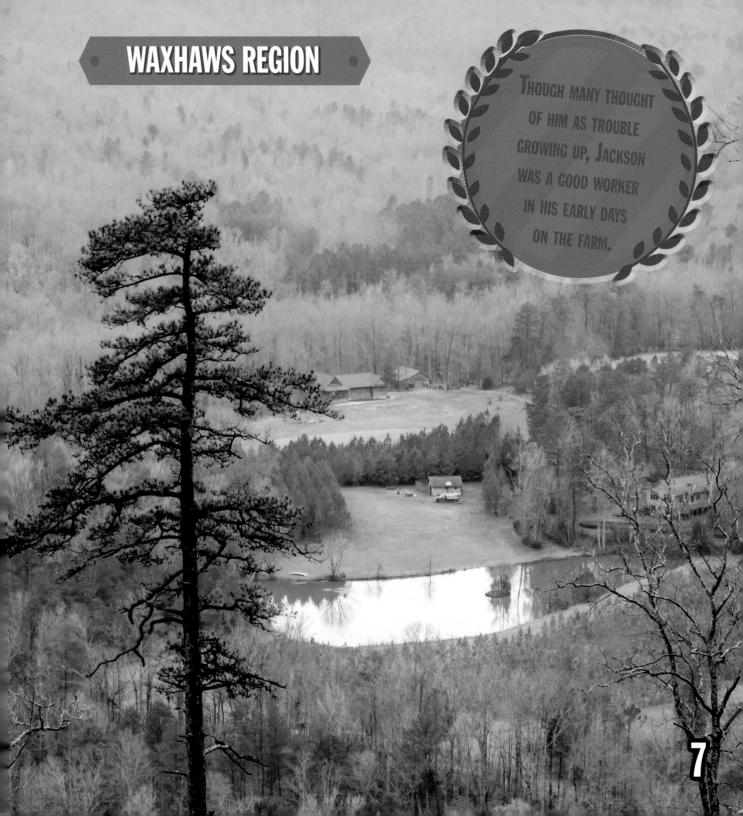

THOUGH MANY THOUGHT OF HIM AS TROUBLE GROWING UP, JACKSON WAS A GOOD WORKER IN HIS EARLY DAYS ON THE FARM.

A BOY IN THE REVOLUTION

By 1776, the American colonies were at war with Great Britain to become an independent nation. When the war made its way to the Waxhaws area of South Carolina, Andrew went off to fight at just 13 years old. He and his brother Robert were captured by the British.

While **captive**, a British officer told Andrew to shine his shoes. When Andrew refused, the officer cut him with a sword. As prisoners, Andrew and Robert both became ill with **smallpox**. Robert died, and Andrew remained sick for many months.

Presidential Preview

The wound from the soldier's sword left Andrew with a white scar, or mark, on his forehead. The scar remained with him for the rest of his life.

JACKSON USED HIS HAND TO BLOCK THE SOLDIER'S SWORD AND HAD HIS FINGERS CUT TO THE BONE.

9

AN IMPORTANT DECISION

Andrew's mother and two brothers died during the American Revolution. Now on his own, he tried being a teacher, even though he had not enjoyed school as a child. Andrew **inherited** some money from a family member in Ireland, but it quickly ran out.

At age 17, Andrew wanted to become a **lawyer**. He moved to North Carolina to study with other successful lawyers. After several years of hard and serious work, he earned the right to practice law.

Presidential Preview

Before she died, Andrew Jackson's mother told him to respect himself and not act in anger. He considered her last words to him to be the "law of [his] life."

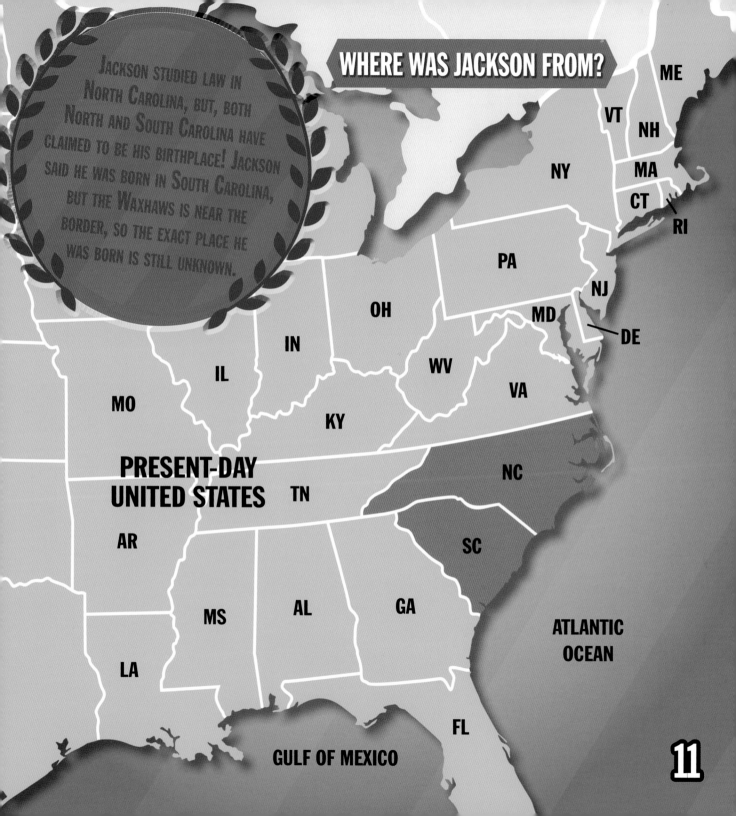

WHERE WAS JACKSON FROM?

Jackson studied law in North Carolina, but, both North and South Carolina have claimed to be his birthplace! Jackson said he was born in South Carolina, but the Waxhaws is near the border, so the exact place he was born is still unknown.

PRESENT-DAY UNITED STATES

ME

VT

NH

NY

MA

CT

RI

PA

NJ

OH

MD

DE

IN

WV

IL

VA

MO

KY

NC

TN

AR

SC

MS

AL

GA

LA

ATLANTIC OCEAN

FL

GULF OF MEXICO

HEADING TO NASHVILLE

After Andrew became a lawyer, his friend and **mentor** John McNairy was made a judge in the western part of North Carolina, which is now Tennessee. He appointed Andrew to be one of his lawyers in 1788. Andrew moved to Tennessee to take the job.

Andrew traveled a rough, wooded trail through Native American territories on his way west to reach Nashville, Tennessee. There, Andrew became known as an honest and hardworking lawyer. He often helped people get back money they were owed.

Presidential Preview

After moving to Nashville, Andrew began buying land and slaves. Over the course of his life, he and his family owned hundreds of slaves. Slavery was the reason for much of his wealth.

In 1796, Andrew Jackson was the first congressman elected in the state of Tennessee, but he resigned after about a year.

13

ONE WIFE, TWO MARRIAGES

In Nashville, Andrew rented a room in the family home of Mrs. Donelson. She had a daughter named Rachel. Rachel was married to a man who made her life unhappy. When Rachel left the man, she moved back into her family's home. There, Rachel and Andrew became close.

The two married in 1791. Both thought Rachel's first husband had **divorced** her, but they later found out that he hadn't. After the divorce was completed, Rachel and Andrew were married again—this time for good—in 1794.

Presidential Preview

Rachel was a sweet and loving wife to Andrew. But terrible things were said about her during Jackson's election. Divorce was uncommon at the time, and many people held her personal life against her.

During Jackson's campaign for president, Rachel became sick. She saw Andrew elected president, but she died of a heart attack before they could move to Washington, DC.

RACHEL JACKSON

A DANGEROUS DUEL

A duel is a fight between two people, often using guns. It's a dangerous way to settle an argument. Andrew was said to have taken part in 103 duels, though it's likely not all of them actually ended with shooting. Some of these disagreements were settled without **conflict**.

At least one did end in gunfire. Charles Dickinson **insulted** Andrew and Rachel, and Andrew wanted to duel. Dickinson fired first and hit Jackson in the chest. Somehow Andrew was still able to take his shot and kill Dickinson.

Presidential Preview

Another time, Andrew was prepared to duel a lawyer named Waightstill Avery. When the time came, both men had calmed down and chose to shoot their guns into the air rather than shoot at each other!

DUELING PISTOL

DESPITE WINNING THE DUEL WITH DICKINSON, JACKSON WAS HURT BADLY. HE DEALT WITH PAIN FROM BEING SHOT FOR THE REST OF HIS LIFE.

AMERICAN HERO

As the War of 1812 began between the United States and Great Britain, Andrew was chosen as the leader of Tennessee's **militia**. He led troops against Native Americans in Alabama and Florida, winning many battles.

By the end of the War of 1812, he had guarded New Orleans, Louisiana, from the British. Because of his successes, Andrew became a popular American hero. His troops even gave him the nickname "Old Hickory" because he was a strong leader.

Presidential Preview

In the Battle of New Orleans, Jackson formed an unusual army that included some regular soldiers, citizens, Native Americans, and even a **pirate!**

WORD SPREAD SO SLOWLY IN 1815 THAT JACKSON DIDN'T KNOW THE WAR HAD OFFICIALLY ENDED MORE THAN 2 WEEKS BEFORE THE BATTLE OF NEW ORLEANS BEGAN!

THE SEVENTH PRESIDENT

In 1804, Jackson bought a large area of land where he built a home called The Hermitage. But he would soon be called from that home. Jackson ran for president in 1824, but lost to John Quincy Adams. Four years later, he became the seventh president of the United States.

Jackson did many things as president, but his life before he took office is one of the most interesting journeys from American citizen to president. Today, people can visit The Hermitage and learn about Jackson's life!

Presidential Preview

The Jacksons didn't have any children of their own. Instead, they raised an adopted son, Andrew Jackson Jr. The Jacksons were also the **guardians** of several other children.

The Early Life of Andrew Jackson

1767	Andrew Jackson is born on March 15.
1779	Jackson's brother Hugh dies in the Battle of Stono Ferry.
1780	Jackson goes off to serve in the American Revolution.
1781	Jackson is captured with his brother Robert and slashed in the face.
1787	Jackson becomes a lawyer.
1796	Jackson is elected to the Tennessee House of Representatives.
1798	Jackson is elected as Tennessee superior court judge.
1802	Jackson is made major general in Tennessee militia.
1804	Jackson buys The Hermitage.
1814	Jackson helps win the Battle of Horseshoe Bend in the War of 1812.
1817	Jackson leads an invasion of Florida in the First Seminole War.
1823	Jackson wins a US Senate seat in Tennessee.
1824	Jackson runs for president, but loses to John Quincy Adams.
1828	Jackson is elected the seventh president of the United States.

ANDREW JACKSON

THE HERMITAGE

GLOSSARY

captive: the state of being kept as a prisoner

conflict: a struggle or fight

divorce: to end a marriage

guardian: a person who is legally appointed to care for another person

inherit: to receive something after a person's death

insult: to say something against another person

lawyer: someone whose job it is to help people with matters related to the law

mentor: someone who provides advice and support to another person

militia: a group of people who only fight when needed

pirate: a person who attacks and steals from ships at sea

resign: to give up a job or position

smallpox: an illness caused by a virus

FOR MORE INFORMATION

Books

Rissman, Rebecca. *Andrew Jackson*. Mankato, MN: Child's World, 2017.

Yomtov, Nel. *Andrew Jackson: Heroic Leader or Cold-Hearted Ruler?* North Mankato, MN: Capstone Press, 2014.

Zuchora-Walske, Christine. *Andrew Jackson's Presidency*. Minneapolis, MN: Lerner Publications, 2017.

Websites

Andrew Jackson
american-historama.org/presidents-united-states/andrew-jackson.htm
Learn about Jackson's life and presidency on this site.

Biography: President Andrew Jackson
ducksters.com/biography/uspresidents/andrewjackson.php
Find out interesting facts about Andrew Jackson and his life here.

The Hermitage
thehermitage.com
Take a virtual tour of Andrew Jackson's Tennessee plantation on this site.

INDEX